Galatians
3:26

Color Isnt

Who I Am

Illustrated by
Mr. Calicreez
with concepts by
Tylesha aka Tye

ISBN 978-1-63885-599-6 (Paperback)
ISBN 978-1-64670-573-3 (Hardcover)
ISBN 978-1-64670-574-0 (Digital)

Covenant Books, Inc.
11661 Hwy 707
Murrells Inlet, SC 29576
www.covenantbooks.com

To YHWH.

I am grateful for my firstborn, Josias Khari Horton, my muse, and to my parents and brother, Claudette, LaKerry Sr., and LaKerry Jr., who encouraged me to pursue writing when despite my passion for it, I had never considered this path until the Holy Spirit inspired my words. I love you!

I may not look like you.
I may not look like them.
But color isn't who I am.

Although my skin may be tan, I'll grow to be a man. A child of *God* is who I AM.

So I'll *love everyone* like me, no matter if it's a he or she. *Human beings* are who *we* be.

Love ALL Humans

1 Cor 3:4-8

it keeps no record Respect of wrongs love is patient love is kind. It does not envy it does not boast it
Kindness Family Forgiving Self-less Trusting
Unconditional Protects perseveres
Forever Caring Generous
Loyalty Honest sweet
Diverse Grace Reliable Meek
Passion Free
Patient
Hope Support Humble
Strength Thankful
Peace

6

Hate and evil do *not* belong! I do not want to stand alone. But even if I'm on my own, the *character* of *Jesus* I will own.

We are *not* defined by color! Even though
we have different mothers, *we must* get
along and live with each other.

American, foreigner, woman or man, blue, black, white, yellow, or tan—color is *not* who I am.

I AM a child of *God*, and so are you.
Everyone else is His children too. Remember,
your color does *not* define you.

We're All H

man Beings

John 3:16

About the Author

Tylesha, aka Tye, is a Navy veteran, a former federal corrections officer, a loving mother, compassionate volunteer for the underprivileged, and an advocate for helping youth to recognize their potential and achieve excellence. Tylesha helps train youth to excel one book at a time through riveting, thought-provoking, age-appropriate literature that helps develop their moral foundations.